Accelerate Your Wealth:

A Comprehensive Guide

to Financial Success

(Unlock the Secrets to Abundance, Prosperity, and Financial Freedom)

By CosmicPrint Publishers

Table of Contents:

Part 1: Setting the Foundation for Financial Success

Introduction: Understanding the Path to Wealth

The journey towards wealth is often perceived as a distant and elusive dream, reserved for a fortunate few or those born into privilege. However, the truth is that wealth is attainable for anyone willing to embark on the path of financial empowerment and disciplined action. In this introduction, we delve into the foundational principles that underpin the pursuit of wealth and prosperity.

At its core, the path to wealth is about more than just accumulating money; it is a journey of self-discovery, empowerment, and purposeful living. Understanding the true essence of wealth requires a shift in mindset, from a focus solely on material possessions to a broader perspective that encompasses financial freedom, fulfillment, and abundance in all aspects of life.

Wealth is not merely a destination but a holistic way of life that encompasses financial stability, personal fulfillment, and a sense of purpose. It is about aligning your values, passions, and goals with your financial decisions to create a life of abundance and prosperity.

Throughout this book, we will explore the practical strategies, mindset shifts, and actionable steps necessary to navigate the path to wealth. By cultivating a deeper understanding of the principles of wealth creation and adopting a mindset of abundance and possibility, you can unlock the doors to financial success and achieve your greatest aspirations.

Chapter 1: Defining Your Financial Goals

Before embarking on any journey, it is essential to have a clear destination in mind. In this chapter, we explore the importance of defining your financial goals and how they serve as the guiding force behind your wealth-building efforts.

Financial goals provide direction and purpose to your financial decisions, helping you prioritize your resources and stay focused on what truly matters to you. Whether your goals include buying a home, starting a business, or achieving financial independence, defining them with clarity and specificity is the first step towards turning your dreams into reality.

When defining your financial goals, it is crucial to consider both short-term and long-term objectives. Short-term goals provide immediate targets for action and progress, while long-term goals offer a vision for the future and guide your overarching wealth-building strategy.

Moreover, your financial goals should be SMART: specific, measurable, achievable, relevant, and time-bound. By setting SMART goals, you create a roadmap for success that is actionable, realistic, and aligned with your values and aspirations.

In addition to setting goals, it is essential to periodically review and reassess them to ensure they remain relevant and aligned with your evolving priorities and circumstances. Flexibility and adaptability are key as you navigate the journey towards wealth, adjusting your goals as needed to stay on course and overcome any obstacles along the way.

Ultimately, defining your financial goals is the first step towards creating a life of abundance and fulfillment. By clarifying your aspirations and committing to their achievement, you set yourself on a path towards financial empowerment and lasting success.

Chapter 2: Crafting a Strategic Plan for Success

Once you have defined your financial goals, the next step is to craft a strategic plan for achieving them. In this chapter, we explore the process of strategic planning and how it enables you to turn your goals into actionable steps and tangible results.

A strategic plan serves as a roadmap for your wealth-building journey, outlining the specific actions, resources, and timelines required to reach your desired outcomes. It provides clarity, direction, and accountability, guiding your decision-making and resource allocation to maximize your chances of success.

When crafting your strategic plan, it is essential to break down your goals into smaller, manageable tasks or milestones. This allows you to track your progress, celebrate your achievements, and stay motivated as you work towards your larger objectives.

Moreover, your strategic plan should consider various factors that may impact your journey towards wealth, including your current financial situation, resources, skills, and external opportunities or challenges. By conducting a thorough analysis of these factors, you can identify potential obstacles and develop contingency plans to mitigate risks and stay on course.

Additionally, your strategic plan should incorporate strategies for both income generation and wealth preservation. This may include diversifying your income streams, investing in assets that generate passive income, and implementing risk management strategies to protect your financial assets.

Throughout the strategic planning process, it is essential to maintain a growth mindset and remain open to new opportunities and possibilities. Flexibility, adaptability, and resilience are key as you navigate the dynamic landscape of wealth creation and pursue your goals with determination and perseverance.

By crafting a strategic plan for success, you empower yourself to take control of your financial future and create the life of abundance and prosperity you desire. With clear goals, actionable strategies, and unwavering commitment, you can turn your dreams into reality and achieve lasting success on the path to wealth.

Chapter 3: Cultivating the Mindset of Wealth

Cultivating a mindset of wealth is the foundation for achieving financial success and abundance. While financial literacy and practical skills are important, it is our beliefs, attitudes, and mindset towards money that ultimately shape our financial destiny. In this chapter, we will explore the key principles and strategies for developing a mindset of wealth, empowering you to overcome limiting beliefs, adopt a prosperity mindset, and achieve your financial goals.

At its core, cultivating a mindset of wealth involves shifting from a scarcity mindset, where there is never enough, to an abundance mindset, where opportunities are limitless and success is attainable. It requires recognizing and challenging the negative beliefs and thought patterns that may be holding you back from achieving your full potential. By reframing your mindset and focusing on abundance, gratitude, and possibility, you can attract wealth and abundance into your life.

One of the fundamental principles of cultivating a mindset of wealth is adopting a positive and empowering attitude towards money and success. Instead of viewing money as scarce or evil, see it as a tool for creating opportunities, empowering yourself and others, and making a positive impact in the world. By embracing a positive mindset and affirming your worthiness and deservingness of wealth and success, you can overcome self-doubt and fears of failure, allowing you to pursue your goals with confidence and determination.

Moreover, cultivating a mindset of wealth involves setting clear and compelling financial goals and visualizing your desired outcomes with clarity and conviction. By defining your vision for financial success and creating a roadmap for achieving your goals, you can focus your energy and attention on the actions and behaviors that will lead to your desired results. Visualization techniques, such as creating vision boards, practicing daily affirmations, and visualizing your success, can help reinforce your beliefs and motivate you to take consistent action towards your goals.

Furthermore, cultivating a mindset of wealth requires taking ownership of your financial decisions and behaviors, and accepting responsibility for your financial situation. Instead of blaming external factors or circumstances for your lack of wealth or success, take proactive steps to educate yourself, improve your financial literacy, and develop the skills and habits necessary for achieving financial independence. By adopting a growth mindset and embracing lifelong learning and personal development, you can empower yourself to overcome obstacles and seize opportunities for growth and advancement.

Additionally, cultivating a mindset of wealth involves surrounding yourself with positive and supportive influences, such as mentors, role models, and like-minded individuals who share your values and aspirations. By seeking guidance and inspiration from those who have achieved success in their own lives, you can learn from their experiences, gain valuable insights and perspectives, and accelerate your own journey towards financial success. Surround yourself with people who uplift and encourage you, and minimize exposure to negative influences or environments that may hinder your progress.

Moreover, cultivating a mindset of wealth involves embracing a mindset of abundance and generosity, and giving back to others in meaningful and impactful ways. By sharing your time, talents, and resources with others, you not only contribute to the greater good but also create a ripple effect of positive energy and abundance in the world. Whether it's through charitable donations, volunteering, mentoring, or supporting causes that align with your values, practicing generosity and gratitude can enhance your sense of fulfillment and purpose, and attract more abundance into your life.

Part 2: Earning Strategies for Rapid Wealth Accumulation

Chapter 4: Leveraging Your Skills and Talents

Your skills and talents are invaluable assets that can serve as powerful catalysts for wealth creation. In this chapter, we explore how to identify, leverage, and monetize your unique abilities to maximize your earning potential and achieve financial success.

The first step in leveraging your skills and talents is to conduct a thorough self-assessment to identify your strengths, interests, and areas of expertise. Take inventory of your skills, both technical and soft, as well as your passions and interests. Consider what sets you apart from others and what unique value you can offer to employers, clients, or customers.

Once you have identified your key strengths and talents, the next step is to explore opportunities to monetize them in the marketplace. This may involve seeking out employment opportunities that align with your skills and interests, freelancing or consulting in your area of expertise, or starting a business based on your unique talents and passions.

In addition to traditional employment, there are numerous avenues for monetizing your skills and talents in today's gig economy. Platforms like Upwork, Fiverr, and TaskRabbit offer opportunities to offer freelance services in a wide range of industries, from graphic design and writing to programming and virtual assistance.

Moreover, consider how you can leverage your skills and talents to create passive income streams that generate revenue even when you're not actively working. This may involve creating and selling digital products, licensing your creative work, or investing in income-generating assets such as rental properties or dividend-paying stocks.

Regardless of the path you choose, the key to success lies in continuously honing and expanding your skills and talents to stay relevant in a rapidly changing marketplace. Invest in ongoing education, training, and professional development to enhance your expertise and increase your earning potential over time.

By leveraging your skills and talents effectively, you can unlock new opportunities for income generation, career advancement, and financial prosperity. Whether you choose to pursue traditional employment, freelance work, entrepreneurship, or passive income streams, your unique abilities are the foundation upon which you can build a life of abundance and fulfillment.

Chapter 5: Exploring Lucrative Career Paths

Choosing the right career path is a critical decision that can significantly impact your earning potential and long-term financial success. In this chapter, we explore various lucrative career paths and strategies for identifying and pursuing opportunities that align with your skills, interests, and goals.

One of the first steps in exploring lucrative career paths is to conduct research and gather information about different industries, occupations, and job markets. Explore trends, growth opportunities, and salary ranges for various professions to gain insights into which careers offer the greatest potential for financial reward and personal fulfillment.

Moreover, consider the intersection of your skills, interests, and values when evaluating potential career paths. Seek out opportunities that align with your passions and strengths, as well as your long-term goals and aspirations. Remember that a fulfilling career is not just about earning a paycheck but also about finding meaning and purpose in your work.

In addition to traditional corporate roles, consider alternative career paths that offer unique opportunities for growth and advancement. Industries such as technology, healthcare, finance, and entrepreneurship often offer high-paying jobs and ample room for career progression.

Furthermore, don't be afraid to think outside the box and explore non-traditional career paths that leverage your skills and interests in innovative ways. With the rise of the gig economy and remote work opportunities, there are more options than ever for pursuing flexible, location-independent careers that offer both financial rewards and lifestyle benefits.

As you explore different career paths, be proactive in seeking out opportunities for networking, mentorship, and professional development. Connect with industry professionals, attend networking events, and seek out mentors who can offer guidance and support as you navigate your career journey.

Ultimately, choosing a lucrative career path is about finding the right balance between financial reward, personal fulfillment, and lifestyle considerations. By taking a strategic approach to career planning and remaining open to new opportunities, you can position yourself for long-term success and achieve your goals of financial independence and prosperity.

Chapter 6: Unlocking Entrepreneurial Opportunities

Entrepreneurship offers unparalleled opportunities for wealth creation, innovation, and personal fulfillment. In this chapter, we explore the process of unlocking entrepreneurial opportunities and turning your business ideas into successful ventures.

The first step in unlocking entrepreneurial opportunities is to identify a viable business idea that aligns with market demand, your skills and interests, and your long-term goals. Conduct market research, analyze industry trends, and identify unmet needs or pain points that your business can address.

Once you have identified a promising business idea, the next step is to develop a comprehensive business plan that outlines your vision, goals, target market, competitive landscape, and financial projections. A well-crafted business plan serves as a roadmap for your entrepreneurial journey, guiding your decision-making and resource allocation as you launch and grow your venture.

In addition to developing a business plan, it is essential to validate your business idea through market testing and feedback from potential customers or clients. Launch a minimum viable product (MVP) or prototype to gauge interest and gather data on customer preferences, pain points, and willingness to pay.

Moreover, consider the various legal, financial, and operational aspects of starting and running a business, such as entity formation, intellectual property protection, accounting and bookkeeping, and sales and marketing strategies. Seek out guidance from legal and financial professionals to ensure compliance and mitigate risks as you navigate the complexities of entrepreneurship.

As you launch and grow your business, be prepared to adapt and pivot in response to changing market conditions, customer feedback, and competitive pressures. Entrepreneurship is a journey filled with challenges and uncertainties, but it also offers limitless opportunities for creativity, innovation, and growth.

By unlocking entrepreneurial opportunities and pursuing your passion for business, you can create a legacy of impact and success while building wealth and financial independence. With determination,

Chapter 7: Maximizing Your Income Streams

In today's dynamic and competitive economy, maximizing your income streams is essential for achieving financial stability, flexibility, and prosperity. Diversifying your sources of income not only increases your earning potential but also provides greater resilience against economic uncertainties and unexpected life events. Whether you're looking to boost your current earnings, pursue new opportunities, or build passive income streams, understanding the strategies for maximizing your income is key to unlocking your full financial potential.

One of the most effective ways to maximize your income streams is to leverage your existing skills, talents, and expertise to pursue additional sources of income. Identify areas where you excel and explore opportunities to monetize your abilities through freelance work, consulting, or teaching. Whether you're a skilled writer, graphic designer, programmer, or marketer, there are countless freelance platforms, job boards, and online marketplaces where you can showcase your talents and connect with clients seeking your services.

Moreover, consider expanding your income streams by diversifying your sources of employment or entrepreneurship. Rather than relying solely on a single job or business venture, explore opportunities to generate income from multiple sources simultaneously. This could involve taking on part-time or freelance work in addition to your full-time job, starting a side business or passion project, or investing in income-producing assets such as rental properties or dividend-paying stocks.

In today's digital age, the internet offers a wealth of opportunities for maximizing your income streams and reaching a global audience. Whether you're selling products, offering services, or creating digital content, the internet provides a platform for monetizing your skills and expertise on a scale that was once unimaginable. Consider launching an online business, selling products on e-commerce platforms, or monetizing your website or social media presence through advertising, affiliate marketing, or sponsored content.

Furthermore, explore opportunities for passive income generation to supplement your active earnings and build long-term wealth. Passive income streams, such as rental income, dividends, royalties, and interest from investments, allow you to earn money with minimal ongoing effort or active involvement. While building passive income streams often requires upfront investment of time, money, or resources, the potential for generating recurring income over time can provide financial security and freedom.

Additionally, consider investing in your education, skills, and personal development to increase your earning potential and open up new opportunities for income growth. Whether it's pursuing advanced degrees, certifications, or specialized training, investing in your knowledge and expertise can enhance your marketability, competitiveness, and earning power in your chosen field or industry. Stay abreast of industry trends, technological advancements, and emerging opportunities to position yourself for success in today's rapidly evolving job market.

Moreover, explore alternative income streams that align with your interests, passions, and values to create a fulfilling and sustainable source of income. Whether it's monetizing your hobbies, talents, or creative pursuits, or exploring unconventional income-generating opportunities such as rental arbitrage, peer-to-peer lending, or online courses, think creatively and outside the box to identify unique ways to maximize your earning potential.

Furthermore, consider leveraging technology, automation, and outsourcing to streamline your income-generating activities and maximize your productivity and efficiency. Whether it's using software tools, apps, or online platforms to automate repetitive tasks, outsource non-core activities, or delegate responsibilities to virtual assistants or freelancers, optimizing your workflow and time management can free up more time and energy to focus on high-impact income-generating activities.

Part 3: Investing for Long-Term Prosperity

Chapter 8: Understanding the Basics of Investing

Investing is a fundamental component of wealth building and financial planning. In this chapter, we delve into the basics of investing, including key concepts, strategies, and principles that every investor should understand.

At its core, investing involves allocating capital with the expectation of generating a return over time. Whether you're investing in stocks, bonds, real estate, or other assets, the goal is to grow your wealth and achieve your financial goals.

One of the first concepts to grasp in investing is the principle of risk and return. Generally, assets with higher potential returns also come with higher levels of risk. Understanding your risk tolerance and investment objectives is essential for constructing a well-balanced investment portfolio that aligns with your goals and preferences.

Moreover, it's crucial to understand the various types of investment vehicles available to investors, including stocks, bonds, mutual funds, exchange-traded funds (ETFs), real estate, and alternative investments. Each asset class has its own risk-return profile, characteristics, and role within a diversified investment portfolio.

Another key aspect of investing is asset allocation, or the strategic distribution of your investment capital across different asset classes based on your risk tolerance, time horizon, and financial goals. By diversifying your investments across multiple asset classes, you can reduce the overall risk of your portfolio while potentially enhancing returns.

Furthermore, investors should understand the importance of asset allocation and rebalancing in maintaining a well-diversified investment portfolio. Periodically reviewing and adjusting your asset allocation based on changes in market conditions and your personal circumstances can help you stay on track towards your financial objectives.

Additionally, investors should be familiar with basic investment strategies, such as dollar-cost averaging, value investing, and growth investing. Each strategy has its own merits and considerations, and the best approach will depend on your individual investment goals and preferences.

Lastly, understanding the role of fees, taxes, and investment costs is essential for maximizing your investment returns over the long term. Be mindful of transaction costs, management fees, and tax implications when making investment decisions, and seek out low-cost investment options whenever possible.

By mastering the basics of investing and adhering to sound investment principles, you can build a solid foundation for long-term financial success and achieve your wealth-building goals.

Chapter 9: Building a Diversified Investment Portfolio

Diversification is a fundamental principle of investing that involves spreading your investment capital across a range of assets to reduce risk and enhance returns. In this chapter, we explore the importance of building a diversified investment portfolio and strategies for achieving optimal diversification.

A diversified investment portfolio is one that includes a mix of asset classes, such as stocks, bonds, real estate, and alternative investments, as well as investments within each asset class that exhibit different risk-return profiles. By diversifying your investments, you can mitigate the impact of market volatility and minimize the risk of significant losses.

One of the primary benefits of diversification is risk reduction. By spreading your investments across multiple asset classes and securities, you can reduce the impact of any single investment or market downturn on your overall portfolio. This can help protect your portfolio from large losses during periods of market turbulence.

Moreover, diversification can also enhance returns by capturing the performance of different asset classes that may perform well under different market conditions. For example, while stocks may outperform bonds during periods of economic expansion, bonds may provide stability and income during market downturns.

When building a diversified investment portfolio, it's essential to consider your investment objectives, risk tolerance, and time horizon. Allocate your investment capital across different asset classes based on your goals and preferences, and periodically rebalance your portfolio to maintain your desired asset allocation.

Additionally, investors should be mindful of correlation among asset classes when diversifying their portfolios. Correlation measures the degree to which the returns of two investments move in relation to each other. Ideally, you want to include assets in your portfolio that have low or negative correlations to each other to maximize diversification benefits.

Furthermore, consider incorporating alternative investments, such as hedge funds, private equity, and commodities, into your portfolio to further diversify your holdings and access unique sources of returns. Alternative investments can provide additional diversification benefits and enhance the risk-adjusted returns of your portfolio.

By building a diversified investment portfolio tailored to your financial goals and risk preferences, you can reduce risk, enhance returns, and achieve greater resilience in the face of market uncertainty. Diversification is a powerful tool for long-term investors seeking to build wealth and achieve financial security.

Chapter 10: Navigating the Stock Market with Confidence

The stock market can be a daunting and volatile environment for investors, but with the right knowledge and strategies, you can navigate it with confidence and achieve your financial goals. In this chapter, we explore key principles and techniques for investing in the stock market successfully.

One of the first steps in navigating the stock market is to develop a solid understanding of how it works and the factors that drive stock prices. Familiarize yourself with basic stock market concepts, such as supply and demand, market trends, and valuation metrics, to make informed investment decisions.

Moreover, take the time to research and analyze individual stocks before investing in them. Evaluate factors such as the company's financial performance, competitive position, industry trends, and management team to assess its investment potential. Conduct thorough due diligence and seek out reliable sources of information to inform your investment decisions.

Additionally, consider adopting a long-term investment approach when investing in the stock market. While short-term market fluctuations and volatility are inevitable, focusing on the underlying fundamentals of the companies you invest in can help you weather market turbulence and achieve sustainable returns over time.

Furthermore, diversification is key to managing risk and optimizing returns in the stock market. Spread your investment capital across a diversified portfolio of individual stocks, mutual funds, and ETFs to reduce the impact of any single investment or market downturn on your overall portfolio.

Another important aspect of navigating the stock market is risk management. Set clear investment objectives and risk tolerance levels, and establish appropriate stop-loss and profit-taking strategies to protect your capital and minimize losses. Additionally, consider using position sizing and asset allocation techniques to manage portfolio risk effectively.

Lastly, stay disciplined and avoid emotional decision-making when investing in the stock market. Maintain a long-term perspective, stick to your investment plan, and resist the temptation to make impulsive trades based on market fluctuations or short-term noise. By staying focused on your investment goals and executing a consistent investment strategy, you can navigate the stock market with confidence and achieve long-term financial success.

Chapter 11: Exploring Alternative Investment Opportunities

In today's dynamic and ever-evolving investment landscape, traditional assets like stocks and bonds are no longer the only options available to investors seeking to diversify their portfolios and achieve attractive returns. Alternative investments have emerged as a compelling and increasingly popular asset class, offering unique opportunities for growth, income, and risk mitigation. In this chapter, we explore the world of alternative investments and the various opportunities they present to investors.

Alternative investments encompass a wide range of asset classes beyond traditional stocks and bonds, including real estate, private equity, hedge funds, commodities, and collectibles. These assets often exhibit low correlation to traditional markets, providing diversification benefits and reducing portfolio volatility. Moreover, alternative investments may offer attractive risk-adjusted returns and income streams that are less reliant on the performance of public markets.

One of the most accessible alternative investments for individual investors is real estate. Real estate investments can take various forms, including residential and commercial properties, real estate investment trusts (REITs), and crowdfunding platforms. Real estate offers the potential for capital appreciation, rental income, and portfolio diversification, making it an attractive option for investors seeking to build wealth and generate passive income.

Private equity is another alternative investment strategy that involves investing in privately-held companies or private equity funds. Private equity investments offer the opportunity to participate in the growth and success of promising startups and established businesses that are not publicly traded. While private equity investments may require a longer investment horizon and higher minimum investment amounts, they can provide attractive returns and portfolio diversification benefits.

Hedge funds are actively managed investment vehicles that employ sophisticated strategies to generate returns while mitigating risk. Hedge funds often use leverage, derivatives, and alternative investment strategies such as long-short equity, global macro, and event-driven investing to achieve their objectives. While hedge funds may be suitable for accredited investors and institutional investors, they can provide diversification and downside protection in volatile market environments.

Commodities are tangible assets that are traded on commodity exchanges and include precious metals, energy products, agricultural goods, and industrial metals. Investing in commodities can provide inflation protection, portfolio diversification, and potential returns that are uncorrelated with traditional financial markets. Moreover, commodities can serve as a hedge against geopolitical risks, supply chain disruptions, and currency fluctuations, making them a valuable addition to a well-diversified investment portfolio.

Collectibles, such as fine art, rare coins, vintage cars, and wine, are another alternative investment option that appeals to investors seeking tangible assets with the potential for appreciation. Collectibles offer the opportunity to invest in unique and culturally significant assets that can appreciate in value over time. While collectibles may require specialized knowledge and expertise to evaluate and acquire, they can provide diversification benefits and aesthetic enjoyment to investors.

In addition to these traditional alternative investments, new opportunities are emerging in the realm of digital assets and cryptocurrencies. Bitcoin, Ethereum, and other cryptocurrencies have gained widespread attention as alternative investment vehicles that offer decentralized, digital forms of value exchange. While cryptocurrencies are highly speculative and volatile, they have the potential to revolutionize the financial system and provide attractive returns for early adopters.

Overall, alternative investments offer compelling opportunities for investors to diversify their portfolios, enhance returns, and mitigate risk. By exploring alternative investment options and incorporating them into a well-balanced investment strategy, investors can position themselves for long-term success and achieve their financial goals in today's complex and dynamic investment landscape.

Part 4: Financial Discipline and Wealth Preservation

Budgeting and saving are foundational pillars of personal finance that form the basis for achieving financial stability, building wealth, and realizing long-term financial goals. In this chapter, we explore the importance of effective budgeting and saving strategies and provide practical tips for managing expenses, increasing savings, and achieving financial security.

Effective budgeting begins with understanding your income, expenses, and financial goals. Start by creating a comprehensive budget that outlines your monthly income sources, including salary, bonuses, and investment income, as well as your fixed expenses such as rent or mortgage payments, utilities, and loan payments. Next, identify discretionary expenses such as dining out, entertainment, and travel, and prioritize your spending based on your financial priorities and goals.

Once you have a clear understanding of your income and expenses, you can begin to implement strategies to reduce expenses and increase savings. Consider cutting unnecessary expenses, negotiating lower rates on recurring bills, and automating savings contributions to ensure consistency and discipline. Set specific savings goals, such as building an emergency fund, saving for retirement, or achieving a specific financial milestone, and allocate a portion of your income towards achieving these goals each month.

In addition to traditional savings accounts, consider leveraging high-yield savings accounts, certificates of deposit (CDs), and other low-risk investment vehicles to maximize the return on your savings while maintaining liquidity and accessibility. Explore tax-advantaged savings vehicles such as employer-sponsored retirement plans like 401(k)s and individual retirement accounts (IRAs) to take advantage of tax-deferred growth and compound interest over time.

It's also important to periodically review and adjust your budget and savings plan as your financial situation evolves and your priorities change. Be proactive in identifying opportunities to optimize your spending, increase your income, and accelerate your progress towards your financial goals. Consider consulting with a financial advisor or using budgeting tools and apps to track your progress and stay on track with your financial plan.

By practicing effective budgeting and saving habits, you can take control of your finances, reduce financial stress, and achieve greater financial security and independence. Remember that small changes in your spending and saving habits can have a significant impact over time, and that building wealth is a marathon, not a sprint. Stay disciplined, stay focused on your goals, and stay committed to your financial success.

Chapter 13: Strategies for Debt Management and Elimination

Debt can be a significant obstacle to financial success and freedom, but with the right strategies and mindset, it is possible to effectively manage and eliminate debt and achieve financial independence. In this chapter, we explore strategies for debt management and elimination, including prioritizing high-interest debt, consolidating debt, and developing a repayment plan.

The first step in debt management is to assess your current debt situation and understand the types of debt you have, including credit card debt, student loans, auto loans, and mortgage debt. Identify which debts have the highest interest rates and prioritize paying off these debts first, as they are costing you the most in interest over time.

Consider consolidating high-interest debt with a balance transfer credit card, personal loan, or home equity line of credit (HELOC) to lower your interest rate and simplify your repayment process. Consolidation can help you save money on interest and reduce the total amount of interest you pay over time, making it easier to pay off your debt faster.

Once you have a clear understanding of your debts and have consolidated high-interest debt where possible, develop a repayment plan that aligns with your financial goals and priorities. Consider using the debt snowball or debt avalanche method to systematically pay off your debts, starting with the smallest balance or highest interest rate debt first, and then rolling those payments into the next debt once each debt is paid off.

In addition to focusing on debt repayment, it's important to avoid accumulating new debt and develop healthy financial habits that support long-term financial stability. Create a realistic budget that prioritizes debt repayment and includes a contingency for unexpected expenses or emergencies. Cut unnecessary expenses, increase your income through side hustles or part-time work, and explore opportunities to reduce your cost of living.

Finally, consider seeking support and guidance from a financial advisor or credit counselor who can provide personalized advice and assistance with debt management and elimination. They can help you develop a customized debt repayment plan, negotiate with creditors on your behalf, and provide strategies for avoiding future debt problems.

By implementing these strategies and staying committed to your debt repayment goals, you can take control of your finances, eliminate debt, and achieve greater financial freedom and security. Remember that debt elimination is a journey that requires patience, perseverance, and discipline, but the rewards of financial independence are well worth the effort.

Chapter 14: Protecting Your Assets and Managing Risk

Protecting your assets and managing risk are essential components of a comprehensive financial plan that safeguard your wealth and ensure your financial security and well-being. In this chapter, we explore strategies for asset protection and risk management, including insurance, estate planning, and diversification.

Insurance is a critical tool for protecting your assets and mitigating financial risk against unforeseen events such as accidents, illnesses, natural disasters, and lawsuits. Consider obtaining various types of insurance coverage, including health insurance, life insurance, disability insurance, homeowners or renters insurance, auto insurance, and umbrella liability insurance, to protect yourself and your loved ones from financial hardship in the event of an emergency or crisis.

Estate planning is another important aspect of asset protection that involves organizing and managing your assets during your lifetime and ensuring their smooth transfer to your heirs and beneficiaries upon your death. Create a will or trust that outlines your wishes regarding the distribution of your assets, appoints guardians for minor children, and designates an executor or trustee to administer your estate. Update your estate plan regularly to reflect changes in your financial situation, family dynamics, and estate planning laws.

Diversification is a key principle of risk management that involves spreading your investments across different asset classes, industries, and geographic regions to reduce the impact of market volatility and minimize the risk of loss. Build a well-diversified investment portfolio that includes a mix of stocks, bonds, real estate, and other asset classes that align with your risk tolerance, investment objectives, and time horizon.

Asset protection also involves minimizing your exposure to liability and litigation risk by structuring your assets in a way that shields them from potential creditors and legal claims. Consider using legal entities such as limited liability companies (LLCs), trusts, and asset protection trusts to protect your personal and business assets from lawsuits, creditors, and other threats.

In addition to insurance, estate planning, diversification, and liability protection, it's important to stay informed about emerging risks and take proactive measures to mitigate them. Monitor your financial accounts regularly, review your insurance coverage annually, and seek professional advice from attorneys, financial advisors, and insurance agents to ensure that your assets are adequately protected and your risk exposure is minimized.

By implementing these strategies and incorporating asset protection and risk management into your overall financial plan, you can safeguard your wealth, protect your loved ones, and achieve greater peace of mind and financial security for the future.

Chapter 15: Cultivating Financial Discipline for Long-Term Success

Financial discipline is the cornerstone of long-term financial success. It involves adopting habits and behaviors that prioritize prudent financial decisions, responsible spending, and strategic saving and investing. Cultivating financial discipline requires dedication, self-awareness, and a commitment to achieving your financial goals despite challenges and temptations along the way.

At its core, financial discipline is about making conscious choices that align with your values, priorities, and long-term aspirations. It requires the ability to resist impulse purchases, delay gratification, and prioritize saving and investing over immediate consumption. While it may seem challenging at first, developing financial discipline is a skill that can be learned and refined over time with practice and perseverance.

One of the first steps in cultivating financial discipline is to create a clear and realistic budget that outlines your income, expenses, and savings goals. A budget serves as a roadmap for your financial journey, helping you track your spending, identify areas where you can cut costs, and allocate resources towards your most important financial objectives. By following a budget consistently, you can develop the discipline to live within your means and avoid overspending.

In addition to budgeting, cultivating financial discipline involves setting specific financial goals and developing actionable plans to achieve them. Whether your goals include paying off debt, saving for a down payment on a home, or building a retirement nest egg, having clear objectives can provide motivation and direction for your financial decisions. Break down your goals into smaller, achievable milestones, and celebrate your progress along the way to stay motivated and focused on your long-term vision.

Another key aspect of financial discipline is practicing frugality and mindfulness in your spending habits. This means being intentional about your purchases, distinguishing between needs and wants, and avoiding unnecessary expenses that detract from your financial goals. Consider adopting strategies such as meal planning, buying in bulk, and negotiating discounts to stretch your dollars further and maximize your savings potential.

Furthermore, cultivating financial discipline requires developing resilience and perseverance in the face of setbacks and obstacles. Financial challenges are inevitable, whether it's unexpected expenses, job loss, or economic downturns. However, by maintaining a positive attitude, staying flexible, and adapting to changing circumstances, you can overcome adversity and stay on track towards your financial goals.

One effective way to reinforce financial discipline is to surround yourself with supportive and like-minded individuals who share your values and goals. Whether it's joining a financial accountability group, seeking guidance from a financial mentor, or engaging with online communities focused on personal finance, having a support network can provide encouragement, accountability, and valuable insights to help you stay disciplined and motivated.

Additionally, cultivating financial discipline involves continuously educating yourself about personal finance topics, investment strategies, and economic trends. By staying informed and proactive, you can make informed decisions that optimize your financial well-being and position yourself for long-term success. Take advantage of resources such as books, podcasts, and online courses to expand your knowledge and skills and empower yourself to make smart financial choices.

Ultimately, cultivating financial discipline is not just about managing money—it's about cultivating a mindset and lifestyle that prioritize financial health, security, and freedom. By embracing discipline, intentionality, and resilience, you can take control of your finances, achieve your goals, and build a brighter financial future for yourself and your loved ones. Remember that financial discipline is a journey, not a destination, and every step you take towards greater financial empowerment brings you closer to realizing your dreams.

www.ingramcontent.com/pod-product-compliance
Lightning Source LLC
Chambersburg PA
CBHW070958290526
45795CB00005B/1694